THE
BIBLE CURE
FOR AFRICA
and the NATIONS

AUTHOR OF *THE IDENTITY THEFT*

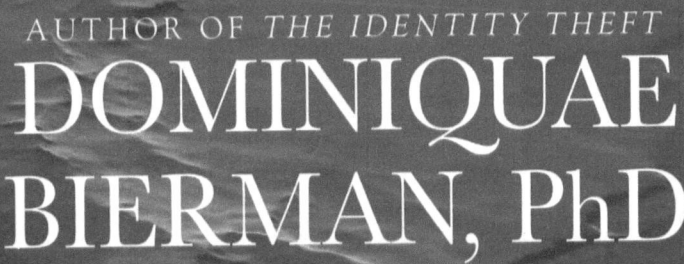

DOMINIQUAE
BIERMAN, PhD

Published by *Zion's Gospel Press*
52 Tuscan Way, Ste 202-412
St. Augustine, FL, 32092
shalom@zionsgospel.com

Paperback ISBN: 978-1-953502-41-4
E-Book ISBN: 978-1-953502-42-1

Printed in the United States of America
First Printing July 2007 in Jerusalem, Second Printing June 2021

ZIONS GOSPEL
PRESS

Thanksgiving

Special thanks go to Archbishop Paul Jubameeta Hackman from Ghana and London, the President of TAPAC (*Trans-Atlantic and Pacific Alliance of Churches*). He gave me an assignment right after I was consecrated as a Bishop in London and Jerusalem. In the First Bishops Forum in Shenandoah Iowa, he asked me to write a proposal of "How can Israel help Africa" It took me two years to come to terms with his request, and finally, the Holy Spirit has given me His heaven-designed title, and with the title, this book was born! Thank you, Archbishop, for challenging me and believing in me enough to trust that I would answer the challenge. You are truly my African father!

CONTENTS

Introduction

Due largely to the effects of the slave trade, colonialism, the international trade regime, geopolitics, corrupt governments, despotism, and constant conflict, Africa is the world's poorest inhabited continent. According to the United Nation's Human Development Report in 2020, the bottom 25 ranked nations (151st to 175th) were mostly all African nations.* (The Next Frontier Human Development and the Anthropocene Human Development Report 2020)

That Africa needs a *cure*, and even an *urgent cure*, is not a new notion. What is new, however, is that the *cure* I am offering in this book *works;* and it will always work because it was given by the Almighty Himself. I will prove to you that there is only *one thing* that must be done in order to turn the entire continent of Africa from the *curse position* to the *blessing position*. There is only *one key* that will activate all the blessings into Africa. It is an ancient key and it never fails. It is very easy to use and implement, but it requires *honesty* and *humility*. It will open the heavens over Africa like nothing else can! It will affect the future governments, and it will propel Africa to a place of financial

* *The Next Frontier Human Development and the Anthropocene Human Development Report 2020.* http://hdr.undp.org/sites/default/files/hdr2020.pdf

superpower. It can be implemented by the smallest of African nations, and it can start with *one person* with *vision*. Elohim, the Creator, always uses the foolish things to confound them that are wise! While the entire world is looking for a solution for Africa, it is right under our noses, in the Holy Book.

The Key of Abraham is the implementation of Genesis 12:3 in what concerns the relationship of all nations and ethnic groups, (families) of the earth; with Abraham's natural descendants, Israel, and the Jewish people. The *blessing* or the *curse* to *every* nation and ethnic group depends on this *one factor*: how the nations have treated Israel and the Jews! History tells us that the relationship with Africa and Israel in the last 40 years has been very problematic. If we study this relationship throughout biblical history, we shall find that it was also problematic even thousands of years ago. This book is being written by the instruction of the Holy Spirit to bring a solution to the problem, and cause an overturning from the *curse* to the *blessing* in all the continent of Africa, and wherever the black race is around the world!

If you are *honest* and *humble*, please take the hand of this Jewish Mother and let me walk you through *truth* so you and your people can be forever *blessed*.

Archbishop Dr. Dominiquae Bierman

President of *Kad-Esh MAP Ministries & United Nations for Israel*

Archbishop of *TAPAC*

Chapter One

A JEWISH WOMAN ARCHBISHOP

I am beginning, on purpose, with some autobiography so that you can get to know me. I am Jewish and accepted the Messiah Yeshua, (Jesus) in a dramatic encounter at the Sea of Galilee. He came to speak to me while guiding a group of Catholic tourists from Mexico in Israel.

He told me, "Run for your life, get baptized, and get saved." I was astounded that Jesus would be speaking to me – a *Jew*. I came from a Jewish Spanish family that was expelled from Spain by the Catholic church during the Spanish Inquisition in 1492. Our history is a history of discrimination and persecution by the nations, for the mere fact that we are Jews.

For the most part, anti-Semitism, or Jewish hatred and discrimination, grew to terrible proportions after the establishment of Christianity as a state religion during the Eastern Roman Empire, (Byzantium,) and the signing of the Council of Nicaea by Emperor Constantine. He separated the original faith in Messiah from anything Jewish and Jews were expelled out of the church in the year 325. He changed the original biblical holidays and Sabbaths into pagan celebrations and established a totally different gospel made in Rome and Babylon, rather than Jerusalem and Zion. This caused the hatred of Jews, and everything Jewish to become the norm and even the duty of the church. Constantine's Christian system affected all of Europe, and Europe affected all of Africa. Thus, the hatred and discrimination of Jews, and blaming Jews for killing Christ, became a reason for persecution, at worst, and secretly despising Jews at best.

Africa's Christianity is an inheritance from Europe's and Constantine's Christianity, not directly from Jerusalem, Israel, nor from the ancient Jewish apostles and prophets. Later on, in the book, we will see why this very important issue has affected the entire continent of Africa. Africa needs a *cure* from European Christianity, and a return to the original Gospel made in Zion, prophesied by Israel's prophets and preached by the 12 Jewish apostles of the Lamb 2,000 years ago!

MY AFRICAN VISION

My husband and I graduated and were ordained to the ministry at CFNI (*Christ for the Nations Bible School*) in Dallas, Texas, on the 7th of May of 1991. A short time afterward, someone told me that they saw me in a vision and that mine was the only white face amidst a "sea of black faces." I treasured that vision in my heart waiting for the time of its fulfillment.

As I pastored in Tel Aviv, Israel, between the years 1998-2004, I came to know many pastors of the foreign African community in Israel. At some point, a large African Christian organization asked me to become the pastor of the Jerusalem African community for this particular organization. I declined the offer since I did not feel it was time yet. Among other people, I met an African evangelist that invited my husband and I to go to Ghana; however, Yahveh (God – "the I AM,") said to me, "The way to Ghana goes through London". Through a series of extraordinary events, I found myself being challenged to become a Bishop through TAPAC (*Trans-Atlantic and Pacific Alliance of Churches*,) as an important step towards my African mission. I had already been accepted and properly announced in the London Gazette when I realized the magnitude of what I was doing.

For a Jew to become a "Christian Bishop" is a very serious issue! We have been persecuted and killed by Christian Bishops ever since Constantine established Christianity as a state religion. Being a woman in ministry in Israel and a senior pastor was already pretty controversial, but becoming a Bishop was like betraying my people altogether. Most Messianic, (Jewish-Christian,) pastors would not understand this. I was setting myself up for *big* trouble! I knew that God had called me, but I would have liked to forget about it! So I delayed my going to London to receive my consecration.

One day, as my husband had the God TV channel on, I saw Reinhard Bonnke ministering to one and a half million people in Nigeria; it was truly "a sea of black faces," a true *ocean*! My spirit was so stirred that I fell on my knees in my private prayer room, crying out before the Father from the depth of my spirit; "What is lacking in me Father in order to answer Your Call to

Africa?" The Holy Spirit told me loud and clear, "You have not gone to London to get your Bishop's title yet." I repented, called London, and in a few days was on a plane with my husband and team. On the 22nd of March of 2004, the original New Moon celebration for the biblical New Year, I was consecrated as a Bishop at the offices and sanctuary of TAPAC in London. On Shabbat, the 19th of June of the same year, Archbishop Hackman and Bishop Susuana Amartefio presided over my public Enthronement Ceremony in Jerusalem at the historical site of the House of Caiaphas, the High Priest during Yeshua's trial prior to His crucifixion.

When I talk about "enthronement" to Africans, they are totally comfortable with it, but when I talk about it to Jewish believers in Messiah, they are very uncomfortable. However, the Israeli non-believers were fascinated by it, and accepted me implicitly, including government authorities. I had to endure their misunderstanding since the Holy Spirit asked me "not to give any explanations." This was His doing and He would show the fruit of it in due time. Since 1996, I have been writing books that would revolutionize the church and the nations. These books are my life message, and they contain the *Key Of Abraham* to sanctify the church from pagan influence and anti-Semitism, and to save the nations. I believe that the *time* has come! It is time to apply THE BIBLE CURE to Africa! The cure is very simple because all biblical solutions are simple! Follow me as we study the "B17 principle" before we can apply *the cure*.

Chapter Two

THE B17 OR "BITTER ALMOND" PRINCIPLE

"So I went to the angel, telling him to give me the little book. And he said to me, "Take it and eat it; it will make your stomach bitter, but in your mouth, it will be sweet as honey."

— **Revelation 10:9**

When I was in my twenties, I opened my first business, it was a health food store. From the first moment that I opened it God blessed it mightily! I had reporters advertising me free of charge. I was a young nursing mother then, that had dared to open her own shop. I loved making people well through healthy nutrition, vitamins, and minerals. Eventually, I became a professional nutritionist and health consultant. Many people were helped and my little shop was frequented by people in distress! I especially loved to cater to those patients that doctors had given up on and had most amazing successes. Two years after my first shop was running and managed as I was pregnant with my second baby, my son, I opened my second health food shop in a city nearby while studying towards my Ph.D. in nutrition and natural health.

Around that time I had discovered that there was a certain vitamin that could help cure terminal cancer patients. This was vitamin B17 or Laetrile. Vitamin B17 is extracted from the bitter almond in the apricot seed. If you have ever cracked an apricot seed and have tried to eat the almond inside, you will never forget the experience. It is one of the bitterest tastes in all of creation! But in the midst of this bitter-tasting almond, there is this wonder vitamin that can actually cure cancer! When someone is dying of cancer, it does not matter if you have to take some bitter medicine. What matters is that bitter or not it can save your life! You may not have any other choice!

I had cancer patients that would frequent my shop asking me for this particular vitamin B17, except I could not help them. This food supplement was forbidden in Israel; no one could sell it legally! After I realized that there were terminal cancer patients that could be rescued if I could obtain this wonder cure, I managed to actually "smuggle" this vitamin from the USA and I would dispense it from under the counter to the very grateful patients that had no other hope! I chose to risk my business rather than risk a guilty conscience for not helping these suffering cancer patients. However, very soon it became known that I had the forbidden medication and "paparachy" like journalists used to try and uncover the sensational story of this woman that was selling the forbidden vitamin, risking her life and career to save patients from certain death! Those were hard days as the media was trying to trap me all the time and more cancer patients were coming over to my shop in hope of purchasing the life-saving vitamin. Finally, I was totally fed up with all the secrecy and persecution! This was a good cause and I had absolutely no fear and shame. Doctors had already given up on these poor patients! I decided to come out in the open and I decorated my shop with all kinds of balloons that were marked with the words B17. Of course, all this came out in the newspapers, but they could never intimidate me again!

Now how would this B17 story apply to this book? I would compare the message of this book to the amazing healing properties of the bitter almond of the apricot. When you chew on it – it can be bitter, but once it begins to take root it effectuates a miraculous cure unmatched by nothing else!

If you realize that Africa needs a miraculous and urgent cure, you then will be very willing and thankful to find this Spiritual B17 in the form of the Message written in the pages of this book!

Even if many would try to intimidate me for distributing this "medication," and you for being willing to receive it, I believe that the importance of rescuing the Continent of Africa is far greater than the possible risk of being controversial and unconventional. I hope and pray that you, dear reader, are made of the stuff that truly great men and women are made and are not afraid to be confronted with the truth so that you and your nation can be healed miraculously!

Here is the spiritual version of B17: THE BIBLE CURE for Africa and the Nations!

Chapter Three

THE BETRAYAL

"Now the sons of Noah who came out of the ark were Shem and Ham and Japheth, and Ham was the father of Canaan. These three were the sons of Noah, and from these, the whole earth was populated."

—Genesis 9:18-19

After Elohim judged the earth with the flood during Noah's times, the whole earth was repopulated from Noah's sons Shem, Ham, and Japheth. The first-born, Shem, was destined to be the forefather of Abraham, through whom Yahveh would bring forth Israel and eventually, the Jewish Messiah, Yeshua (Jesus). Shem means "name" in Hebrew, and indeed the Almighty was going to exalt His Holy name through Shem and his descendants Abraham, Isaac, Jacob,

Judah, and the people of Israel. He also promised to make the name of Abraham, Shem's descendant, great! In fact, his name is so great that most people in the world know Abraham's name and of course, the name of Israel. The name Israel is mentioned over 2000 times in the Holy Scriptures, (the Bible,) and it is the second-most mentioned name besides Yahveh and Elohim, the I Am and the Creator.

"Now the LORD said to Abram, "Go forth from your country, And from your relatives and from your father's house to the land which I will show you; and I will make you a great nation, and I will bless you, and make your name great; and so you shall be a blessing; and I will bless those who bless you, and the one who curses you I will curse and in you all the families of the earth will be blessed."

— Genesis 12:1-3

These verses above are so foundational that they actually determine all of the histories of mankind from that moment forward! The salvation and blessing of every nation and family on the earth, (ethnic group or race,) would depend on their attitude and behavior towards Abraham's natural seed, namely, the people of Israel and the Jewish people of today. The covenant made with Abraham is irrevocable and it will stand forever.

"He has remembered His covenant forever, the Word which He commanded to a thousand generations, the covenant which He made with Abraham, and His oath to Isaac. Then He confirmed it to Jacob for a statute, to Israel as an everlasting

covenant, saying, "To you, I will give the land of Canaan as the portion of your inheritance," when they were only a few men in number, very few, and strangers in it. And they wandered about from nation to nation, from one kingdom to another people. He permitted no man to oppress them, and He reproved kings for their sakes: Do not touch My anointed ones, and do My prophets no harm."

— Psalms 105:8-15

The covenant made with Israel through Abraham includes a land, a promised land, a holy land, that used to be called Canaan. It was from the River Nile in Egypt to the River Euphrates in ancient Assyria and modern-day Iraq.

"On that day the LORD made a covenant with Abram, saying, "To your descendants, I have given this land, from the river of Egypt as far as the great river, the river Euphrates"

— Genesis 15:18

The entire modern-day "political conflict" over Israel is nothing but a "biblical conflict" between those nations that support Israel's right to settle in the whole land promised to Abraham, and between those nations that are opposing the will of God Almighty on this issue. Therefore, whoever will oppose Yahveh on this the issue will find himself His enemy. Every nation that opposes the plan of Yahveh to reestablish His Jewish people in their ancient land comes to disgrace.

"O God, do not remain quiet; Do not be silent and, O God, Do not be still. For behold, your enemies make an uproar, and those who hate You have exalted themselves. They make shrewd plans against your people and conspire together against Your treasured ones. They have said, "Come, and let us wipe them out as a nation, that the name of Israel be remembered no more." For they have conspired together with one mind; against You, they make a covenant"

— Psalms 83:1-5

In the "Palestinian" books of learning and in their maps, the name of Israel does not exist. They call the Land of Abraham "Falestin." Those that side with the "Palestinian cause" are promised judgment, tempests, storms, shame, and humiliation (which includes poverty!).

"So pursue them Your tempest and terrify them with Your storm. Fill their faces with dishonor, that they may seek Your name, O LORD, let them be ashamed and dismayed forever, and let them be humiliated and perish."

— Psalms 83:15-17

The promise against Yah's, (God's,) enemies in this is total destruction:

"And it will come about that after I have uprooted them, I will again have compassion on them; and I will bring them back, each one to his inheritance and each one to his land. "Then if they will really learn the ways of My people, to swear by My name, 'as Yahveh lives,' even as they taught My people to swear by Baal, they will be built up in the midst of My people. "But if they will not listen, then I will uproot that nation, uproot and destroy it," declares Yahveh."

— Jeremiah 12:14-17

Whoever divides the land of Israel to give it away to Israel's enemies enters into the Valley of Yehoshapahat, (God's judgment):

"For behold, in those days and at that time, when I restore the fortunes of Judah and Jerusalem, I will gather all the nations and bring them down to the valley of Jehoshaphat. Then I will enter into judgment with them there on behalf of My people and My inheritance, Israel, whom they have scattered among the nations; and they have divided up My land. "They have also cast lots for My people, traded a boy for a harlot, and sold a girl for wine that they may drink."

— Joel 3:1-3

Most nations that have preferred the favor of the Arab oil, rather than the favor of Yahveh, are in dire straits today. That can be seen in the continent of Africa. Not only that, since the USA has put her hand to divide the land of Israel and to establish a Palestinian state, it has suffered from the most terrible catastrophes in her history. The ones that stand out the most are the destruction of the Twin Towers on 9/11, 2001, exactly 24 hours after the US had signed an agreement with the Saudi Arabian ambassador, Mr. Bandar, in order to establish a

Palestinian state in Israel. Also, Hurricane Katrina destroyed areas of Louisiana, Mississippi, and Alabama in August of 2005, and hit ground *exactly* on the day the Gaza Disengagement ended; the uprooting of nearly 10,000 hard-working Jews from biblical land that they had made bloom on sand dunes with sweat and blood. I suggest that you read my book "Stormy Weather" where I have proven beyond a shadow of a doubt that there is a direct connection between escalation of terror, terrible storms, and Global Warming and between the judgments of Elohim against the nations because of the "cause of Zion."

"Draw near, O nations, to hear; and listen, O peoples! Let the earth and all it contains hear, and the world and all that springs from it. For the LORD'S indignation is against all the nations, and His wrath against all their armies; He has utterly destroyed them, He has given them over to slaughter... For the LORD has a day of vengeance, a year of recompense for the cause of Zion."

— Isaiah 34:1-2, 8

He is not only judging those who have actively opposed or harmed Israel, but He is doing the same with those who have stood by passively, ignoring Israel's suffering and do nothing to help her. He is judging, at present, both sins of omission and sins of the commission concerning Israel.

"Because of violence to your brother Jacob, You will be covered with shame, and you will be cut off forever. "On the day that you stood aloof, on the day that strangers carried off his wealth, and foreigners entered his gate and cast lots for Jerusalem, you too were as one of them.... For the day of the LORD draws near on all the nations as you have done, it will be done to you, your dealings will return on your own head."

— Obadiah 10-11, 15

The nations have truly "sold a girl for wine that they might drink". They wanted to "drink" petrol dollars and Arab oil, but instead of this they are drinking the "wine of judgment." Unfortunately, Africa has played the "harlot" concerning Israel and it has betrayed Israel many times since its inception. The list of betrayals for the purpose of financial favor from the Arabs is so long and painful that there is an entire book written about it called, "Israel and Africa: the Problematic Friendship" by Joel Peters. In his book, published in 1992, Peters says:

Israel's relations with Africa began over thirty years ago (45 years now in 2007.) with the achievement of independence by the African States. In many cases, contacts were established with African leaders before decolonization. No sooner had Ghana become independent in 1957, then Israel opened its first embassy in Africa. In the ensuing years, Israel befriended the new African states, creating an extensive network of relations on the continent. The 1960s were a period in Israeli-African relations characterized by a spirit of friendship, Israel's relations with Africa began over thirty years ago (45 years now in 2007.) with achievement and cooperation. Israel succeeded in establishing relations with thirty-three states and signed cooperation treaties with twenty-two of them. A series of visits by both sides helped consolidate the growing relationship. Jerusalem soon became a regular and important stop on the diplomatic itineraries of African leaders.

The most prominent aspect of Israeli African relations during these years was the development of Israeli aid programs. *Israel sent hundreds of experts to work on a variety of projects in Africa. Its efforts were not confined to a few countries; Israelis were to be found throughout the continent.* Israel soon became a much sought-after donor of aid in Africa, with requests for training far outstripping the country's limited resources. *(Let us remember that Israel rose from the ashes of the Nazi Holocaust, and 2000 years of exile and suffering with no help from the nations!)*

Through its activities in Africa, Israel gained friendship and a positive image in the world. In short, Israel was dramatically catapulted out of its diplomatic isolation.

This friendship proved to be short-lived. Like Israel, the Arabs also sought to maximize their influence in Africa. Africa quickly became a diplomatic battleground between Israel and Arabs for political support. After Israel's victory in the Six-Day War in June 1967 (40 years ago! In 2007 D.B.), *the Africans became increasingly critical of Israel and supportive of the Arab cause.* The steady decline in Israel's position in Africa reached its low point during the Yom Kippur War in October of 1973 when the African states in rapid succession, rushed to renounce their friendship with

Israel and broke off diplomatic relations. By the end of the war, only four states had not joined the bandwagon.

The severing of diplomatic relations did not signify a complete Israeli disengagement from Africa. Although the break resulted in the immediate withdrawal of the aid programs, a new set of profitable commercial links were developed in their stead. At the political level, however, contacts were sporadic and of little consequence. For several years, there was an absence of any systematic policymaking in Jerusalem toward relations with Africa. Israel made little attempt to restore its former position in the continent. Likewise, for the Africans, the question of relations with Israel ceased to be an important issue. (End of quote)

Modern-day Israel has sought to do well to Africa and pursued it actively until Africa betrayed Israel during the Six-Day War and the Yom Kippur War. In both cases, Israel was not the attacker, but rather was attacked by its Arab neighbors that greatly outnumbered her! She could have been annihilated, but Yahveh sustained her and gave her more territory according to the covenant made with Abraham. Africa, which had been so blessed by the financial aid programs of young reborn Israel, repaid good with evil, and since then it has been in abject poverty and humiliation. The eternal Word of God says that when someone repays evil for good, evil will never leave his house.

"He who returns evil for good, evil will not depart from his house."

— Proverbs 17:13

Not long ago I had a divine appointment with an African church leader that had been in politics in his nation; He had even run for the presidency and lost. After many years of pondering what was missing in order for God to bless his African nation, the Holy Spirit spoke to him and said that what was lacking was making restitution to Israel. This "issue of restitution" is the KEY issue for the overturning of the situation in Africa. Until today, 2007, though some relationships have been reestablished between Israel and African countries, not one of them has his embassy in Jerusalem, and no restitution has been made.

When Great Britain betrayed Israel by breaking the promise made by LORD Balfour and the Queen in the *Balfour Declaration* of 1917 to establish a Jewish national home in the land that is called today Israel, it lost its vast empire. By 1948, (the War of Independence of Israel and the end of the British Mandate in the Holy Land,) Great Britain was retreating from most of its colonies. "The sun never set on the British Empire," is no more a reality because they betrayed the Jewish people.

Even before Israel became a national entity in its land after 2,000 years of exile, when Zionism was in its beginning steps, the leader and prophet of the restoration of Israel, Mr. Theodor Herzl, declared,

"Once I have witnessed the redemption of the Jews, my people, I wish also to assist in the redemption of the Africans." (Theodore Herzl, *Die Alteneuland,* 1902)

Our first female Prime Minister, the legendary Golda Meir wrote,

"I am prouder of Israel's International Cooperation Programme and of the technical aid that we gave to the people of Africa than I am of any other single project we have ever undertaken." (Golda Meir, *My Life,* 1975)

The Jewish people have always had a great love and appreciation for Africa: Unfortunately, the response of Africa and Ham has not always been righteous. Elohim said to Abraham and his descendants, the Jewish people:

"And I will bless those who bless you, and the one who curses you I will curse, and in you, all the families of the earth will be blessed."

— Genesis 12:3

As I continue exposing the roots of disease and poverty in Africa, please keep your heart humble. All good doctors must diagnose the root cause of the disease before applying the cure. The Word of God warns us not to apply superficial treatment to a wound. Please bear with me and with the help of the Father in heaven, as I proceed to bring forth real balm for the salvation and the restoration of Africa.

"They have healed the brokenness of My people superficially, Saying, 'Peace, peace,' but there is no peace." Were they ashamed because of the abomination they have done? They were not even ashamed at all; they did not even know how to blush. Therefore they shall fall among those who fall; at the time that I punish them, they shall be cast down," says the LORD."

— Jeremiah 6:14, 15

True healing always involves repentance and restitution. We will speak about the cure after we expose and disinfect the wound. For that purpose, we need to study Africa's relationship with Israel throughout the Bible. Let us meet Ham, the second son of Noah.

Chapter Four

HAM & AFRICA

"Now this is the genealogy of the sons of Noah: Shem, Ham, and Japheth. And sons were born to them after the flood. The sons of Ham were Cush, Mizraim, Put, and Canaan."

— Genesis 10:1,3

A ll civilization comes from these three sons of Noah. It is clear from the Scriptures and from historical evidence that Ham was the father of the black race. Mizraim translated as "Egypt" and Egypt is also called the land of Ham. (Psalms 105:23)

The historian, Herodotus, who is regarded by scholars as the "Father of History," wrote somewhere between 475 to 450 BC, "The Colchians, Ethiopians, and Egyptians have thick lips, broad nose, wooly hair and they are burnt off skin" Of course the Sphinx in Giza displays all those qualities. In other words, the ancient Egyptians were not white, but rather black and all of Ham's sons were black.

In Hebrew, the word for "Ethiopian" is *cushi*, which also means a person of black skin.

"Can the Ethiopian (a Cushi a person of black skin) change his skin or the leopard its spots? Neither can you do good who are accustomed to doing evil."

— Jeremiah 13:23

In order to understand the past and the future of Africa, and the entire black race, we must take an *honest* look at history and especially biblical history. We will discover that Ham was designed for greatness and so all the black race with him; however, he missed the mark from the beginning. With honesty and humility let *us learn from the mistakes of the past so that Africa can become GREAT as Elohim designed her to be!*

Let us take a look at the history of Ham's descendants.

"Then Noah began farming and planted a vineyard. He drank of the wine and became drunk, and uncovered himself inside his tent. Ham, the father of Canaan, saw the nakedness of his father and told his two brothers outside. But Shem and Japheth took a garment and laid it upon both their shoulders and walked backward and covered the nakedness of their father; and their faces were turned away so that they did not see their father's nakedness. When Noah awoke from his wine, he knew what his youngest son had done to him. So he said,

"Cursed be Canaan; a servant of servants He shall be to his brothers." He also said, "Blessed be Yahveh, the God of Shem; and let Canaan be his servant. "May God enlarges Japheth, and let him dwell in the tents of Shem, and let Canaan be his servant."

— Genesis 9:20-27

This is the first biblical account of Ham and his activities. We can see that he was not careful to *honor* his father, Noah, and that incurred a curse that affected his son, Canaan. Canaan was the father of all the Canaanites (all the Jebusites, Amorites, Hittites, etc.) that Yahveh told Joshua to completely annihilate in order to possess the Promised Land. Only a few were left, but they became Israel's slaves just like Genesis 9:27 states.

In Genesis 10 we meet another descendant of Ham, this is Nimrod.

"Now Cush became the father of Nimrod; he became a mighty one on the earth. He was a mighty hunter before the LORD; therefore it is said, "Like Nimrod a mighty hunter before the LORD." The beginning of his kingdom was Babel and Erech and Accad and Calneh, in the land of Shinar."

— Genesis 10:8-10

Cush beget Nimrod, and Nimrod was a master builder and he built the Tower of Babel. He must have had some amazing administration skills! Nimrod was a religious man; he wanted to reach God but he tried in the wrong way!

"Now the whole earth used the same language and the same words. It came about as they journeyed east, that they found a plain in the land of Shinar and settled there. They said to one another, "Come, let us make bricks and burn them thoroughly." And they used brick for stone, and they used tar for mortar. They said, "Come, let us build for ourselves a city and a tower whose top will reach into heaven, and let us make for ourselves a name, otherwise we will be scattered abroad over the face of the whole earth." The LORD came down to see the city and the tower which the sons of men had built. Yahveh said, "Behold, they are one people, and they all have the same language. And this is what they began to do, and now nothing which they purpose to do will be impossible for them. "Come, let Us go down and there confuse their language so that they will not understand one another's speech." So Yahveh scattered them abroad from there over the face of the whole earth, and they stopped building the city. Therefore its name was called Babel because there the LORD confused the language of the whole earth; and from there the LORD scattered them abroad over the face of the whole earth."

— Genesis 11:1-9

Under the leadership of Nimrod, all the inhabitants of the earth rallied to build the Tower of Babel. Not only was Nimrod an amazing administrator, he must have been a tremendously charismatic leader. He started the first One World Order and Religion – Babylon! Babylon was established by a descendant of Ham, just like Egypt, (Mizraim in Hebrew,) was established by the son of Ham. So the two most ancient civilizations were established by black people, descendants of Ham. That tells us that *the black race is endowed with some astounding capabilities and gifts and all of Africa should be a superpower!* Culture and civilization started with Babel, (Nimrod,) and Mizraim, (Egypt). *The black race should have no inferiority complex* and should be leading in every arena! What caused its downfall from the beginning?

1. Ham's dishonoring of His Father Noah; brought about the curse of Canaan.

2. Religious pride against the Creator: They said,

"Come, let us build for ourselves a city and a tower whose top will reach into heaven, and let us make for ourselves a name, otherwise we will be scattered abroad over the face of the whole earth."

— Genesis 11:4

Lucifer, who is now called Satan, also fell because of pride. Pride is a very dangerous disease. Entire civilizations have crumbled and fallen apart because they lifted themselves in pride against the Almighty; Babylon, Persia, Greece, Rome, and very soon Islam. Any group of people that lifts itself above Yahveh and His plans is destined to lose footing and be cast down! When Israel as a nation refused to follow the Messiah, Israel was exiled out of the Land for 2,000 painful and very long years!

"Pride goes before destruction, and a haughty spirit before a fall."

— Proverbs 16:18

IMPORTANT FACTS

The first city that Elohim fought against was Babel, built by black Nimrod, and the first cities that He destroyed were Sodom and Gomorra, both Canaanite (from Ham!) cities. They were destroyed because of sexual immorality and especially homosexuality. Today, the number one problem of Africa and the highest mortality rate is due to AIDS, which is, for the most part, contracted due to sexual promiscuity and most particularly, homo-sexuality. (See Genesis 13:10, Genesis 18:20, and Genesis 19.) Today, AIDS is the number one killer in Africa!

Chapter Five

ISRAEL & AFRICA
– AN ANCIENT HISTORY

"And I will bless those who bless you, and the one who curses you I will curse, and in you, all the families of the earth will be blessed."

— Genesis 12:3

W e can see that the Bible mentions the history of Ham prior to the history of Shem, the father of Abraham and Israel, but when it comes to covenant order we must start with Abram. Elohim chose Abram. Abram answered the call to become the father of many nations, under whom the entire world would be turned back to the worship of the one true God -Yahveh, the Creator. God chose

Abram to start a "chosen people" unto Himself through whom He would work His plan of redemption, and the Messiah, the anointed King of the Jews and the world savior would come! In order to protect His plan and order He promised Abraham a few things:

"Now the LORD said to Abram, "Go forth from your country, and from your relatives and from your father's house to the land which I will show you; and I will make you a great nation, and I will bless you, and make your name great; and so you shall be a blessing"

— Genesis 12:1-2

By the mere fact that Elohim promised all the natural descendants of Abraham would become great and blessed, in order to protect His chosen nation, He said:

"And I will bless those who bless you, and the one who curses you I will curse, and in you, all the families of the earth will be blessed."

— Genesis 12:3

Whoever would bless and honor those that Yahveh chose would be in return blessed and honored. Whoever from the nations would dishonor and curse them, Yahveh would totally destroy!

In Hebrew there are two words for *curse* mentioned here:

1. Klala – to take lightly and to dishonor
2. Meera – to utter a decree of total destruction

From then on, the future of the nations would depend on how they relate to the natural descendants of Abraham – Israel and the Jewish people. By honoring them as one would honor a father or a mother, nations would be honoring the Almighty Himself who chose them, and His plan of redemption for ALL mankind. Both history and the Holy Scriptures prove this point. All the empires that rose against Israel have disappeared! (Where are Babylon, Persia, Assyria, Egypt, Greece, and Rome? They are not empires nowadays!)

"Draw near, O nations, to hear; and listen, O peoples! Let the earth and all it contains hear, and the world and all that springs from it. For the LORD'S indignation is against all the nations, and His wrath against all their armies; He has utterly destroyed them, He has given them over to slaughter...For Yahveh has a day of vengeance, a year of recompense for the cause of Zion."

— Isaiah 34:1-2, 8

"For the day of Yahveh draws near on all the nations. As you have done, it will be done to you, your dealings will return on your own head."

— Obadiah 15

"For thus says Yahveh of hosts, "After glory, He has sent me against the nations which plunder you, for he who touches you, touches the apple of His eye."

— Zechariah 2:8

"For behold, in those days and at that time, when I restore the fortunes of Judah and Jerusalem, I will gather all the nations And bring them down to the valley of Jehoshaphat. Then I will enter into judgment with them there on behalf of My people and My inheritance, Israel, whom they have scattered among the nations; and they have divided up My land. "They have also cast lots for My people, traded a boy for a harlot, and sold a girl for wine that they may drink."

— Joel 3:1-3

The biblical history between the black race and Israel is quite complex.

ISAAC & ISHMAEL

"Now Sarai, Abram's wife had borne him no children, and she had an Egyptian maid whose name was Hagar. So Sarai said to Abram, "Now behold, the LORD has prevented me from bearing children. Please go into my maid; perhaps I will obtain children through her." And Abram listened to the voice of Sarai. After Abram had lived ten years in the land of Canaan, Abram's wife Sarai took Hagar the Egyptian, her maid, and gave her to her husband Abram as his wife. He went into Hagar, and she conceived; and when she saw that she had conceived, her mistress was despised in her sight."

— Genesis 16:1-4

We can see that Hagar, a black Egyptian lady, was a servant to Sarai, Abram's wife. She was being elevated in her position in the family by conceiving to Master Abram. But the ancient sin of Ham came upon her, pride rose within her, and she despised the mother of faith, Sarah!

Elohim had mercy on Hagar, on behalf of Abraham's son in her womb, and promised to multiply her offspring if she went back to her mistress in total submission! Hagar could have died, and so would Ishmael, but "submitting to authority" and honoring Yah's order saved the lives of Hagar and Ishmael.

So, we know that Ishmael was half black. It is also a fact that Islam, and through it the hatred and the despising of Israel, is ruling large areas of Africa. Islam is based on the lie that the promised son of Abraham, whom he attempted to sacrifice on Mount Moriah, was Ishmael, and not Isaac. Therefore, all of Islam is bent on destroying ISAAC'S descendants and on occupying the land promised to Abraham, Isaac, and Jacob as an inheritance.

"He has remembered His covenant forever, the Word which He commanded to a thousand generations, the covenant which He made with Abraham, and His oath to Isaac. Then He confirmed it to Jacob for a statute, to Israel as an everlasting

covenant, saying, "To you, I will give the land of Canaan as
the portion of your inheritance,"

— Psalms 105:8-11

Islam, in Africa with its pro-Palestinian approach, has been
affecting the politics of the continent, and with it, the condition
of all of its inhabitants according to the promise and the warning
of Genesis 12:3.

JOSEPH & PHARAOH IN EGYPT

Joseph, the son of Jacob and Rachel, was sold to slavery by his
brothers and ended in Egypt where, after great success in his job,
was accused falsely by his mistress that tried to rape him. He
landed in jail where he rose to prominence and became the head
of all the prisoners. Here he showed excellence and ministered
in the gift of Prophecy, which eventually brought him before
the (black!) Pharaoh. When Joseph interpreted the dreams of
Pharaoh and rightly predicted the coming seven years of famine,
Pharaoh honored him and made him second in his kingdom.
Israeli Joseph administered all of Egypt and under him, Egypt
prospered above all other nations. Pharaoh gave Joseph an
Egyptian (black) wife, Asenath, daughter of Potiphera the
priest of On, and she bore him two sons, Menashe and Ephraim
that were half-black and half-white or olive skin. Eventually,
Ephraim became the ruling tribe of the northern kingdom of
Israel that was later exiled to Assyria in the 8th century BC
and was scattered among all the nations. These are the "10 lost

tribes." Ephraim was a son of a mixed marriage between Ham, (Egyptian Asenath,) and Shem, (Israeli Joseph). Thus, the history between Ham and Israel continues...

MOSES & EGYPT

Eventually, Joseph's brothers came to Egypt for help and there was a family reunion. Joseph sent for Jacob, his father, and Benjamin, his brother, and all of Israel to relocate to Egypt during the seven years of famine. While Joseph was alive, Pharaoh was kind to the Israelites, but when Joseph died another (black) Pharaoh came to power and he was cruel to the Israelites and used them as slaves. Thus, the curse of Genesis 12:3 is put in motion concerning Egypt. Moses, a Levite, is raised in the courts of Pharaoh when his family saved him as a newborn babe from the fate that awaited all Israelite boys - murder. In order to subdue the people, Pharaoh ordered all the newborn male children of Israel to be killed. Moses was put in a basket in the Nile River, and the daughter of Pharaoh found him believing that the "Nile god" had given her a child and she raised him as an Egyptian. When Moses grew up he discovered his Israelite identity, tried to fight for his people by killing one of the Egyptian slave masters. In fear, he fled to the desert and ended up at the tent of Jethro, the Priest of Midian, (also black, a descendant of Keturah and Abraham Genesis 25:1-2). Moses married Zipporah, the eldest daughter of Jethro. Zipporah was also black and she bore Moses two sons that were half-Ham and half- Shem (Israel).

"Miriam and Aaron began to talk against Moses because of his Cushite wife, for he had married a Cushite."

— Numbers 12:1

As I have mentioned before, a "Cushite or a Cushi" means a black person and is derived from Ham's son, *Cush*. So we know that Moses' wife was a black lady.

Moses returns to Egypt after a powerful encounter with Yahveh, the great "I Am" at the burning bush in Mount Horeb. He returns as the deliverer of Israel. Pharaoh hardens his heart and refuses to let Israel GO. Ten plagues later, after Pharaoh's first-born dies, he chases Israel out of Egypt begging Moses to bless him! However, he changes his mind very quickly and when Israel is stuck between the desert and the Red Sea, Pharaoh's chariots charge against the fleeing Israelites. Through an awesome, powerful move, the Almighty opens the Red Sea, His people, Israel, cross on dry land, and when the Egyptian chariots touch the waters, the waters return and drown the entire Egyptian Army. Thus, all the might of Egypt is destroyed, never to rise again! The curse of Genesis 12:3 comes to pass and it is so until this day!

JETHRO-HOBAB'S GOLDEN OPPORTUNITY

Jethro, whose name is also Hobab, came to visit Moses, his son-in-law, in the Sinai desert. He had heard about the mighty things Elohim had done for Moses and Israel and wanted to congratulate him. Jethro had the administration skills of Ham, (through his foremother Keturah,) and helped Moses establish the system of leadership in the desert. I do not know what Moses would have done without his black father-in-law! Moses knew that he needed help and wisdom, so he asked Hobab (Jethro) to stay with him and help him. He even promised Hobab that all the promises Elohim had given to Israel would be his as well. He invited his father-in-law to become part of the family of Israel and to receive all of its inheritance in exchange for some PRACTICAL HELP, but Hobab refused this amazing offer! Later, the Midianites became the archenemies of Israel and sent Balaam to curse it. Israel ends up destroying all the Midianite cities! If only Jethro would have been a little bit more humble and less selfish, all of Midian would have been blessed! (Numbers 22 and 31) Again, we can see the curse of Genesis 12:3 coming into full effect because Jethro refuses to help Moses and despises the offer of becoming ONE with Israel under the leadership of Moses. Could it be that he did not like to be under the rule of Israel? After all, he was *the* Priest of Midian and must have liked his position; maybe it was jealousy? Whatever the reason, it was wrong and Biblical history shows it clearly.

In Deuteronomy 23 we can see that Yahveh utters the curse of Genesis 12:3 on all those that refused to help Israel in the desert:

"No Ammonite or Moabite shall enter the assembly of the LORD; none of their descendants, even to the tenth generation, shall ever enter the assembly of the LORD, because they did not meet you with food and water on the way when you came out of Egypt, and because they hired against

you Balaam the son of Beor from Pethor of Mesopotamia, to curse you. "Nevertheless, the LORD your God was not willing to listen to Balaam, but the LORD your God turned the curse into a blessing for you because the LORD your God loves you. You shall never seek their peace or their prosperity all your days."

— Deuteronomy 23:3-6

ISRAEL & CANAAN

When the children of Israel arrive in Canaan after 40 long years in the desert, they are given a command to annihilate all of the Canaanites. Canaan was the son of Ham that Noah cursed because of dishonoring his father and uncovering his nakedness (Genesis 9).

"For My angel will go before you and bring you into the land of the Amorites, the Hittites, the Perizzites, the Canaanites, the Hivites, and the Jebusites; and I will completely destroy them. "You shall not worship their gods, nor serve them, nor do according to their deeds, but you shall utterly overthrow them and break their sacred pillars in pieces."

— Exodus 23:23,24

So Israel inherits the land of Canaan, the son of Ham. In that sense, the land of Israel should be part of Africa, just like Egypt is part of Africa. But Shem inherits it through the children of Abraham, the nation of Israel.

The Philistines, Israel's archenemies, are descendants of Ham through Mizraim.

King Solomon & Queen of Sheba – a Blood Connection?

"She gave the king a hundred and twenty talents of gold and a very great amount of spices and precious stones. Never again did such abundance of spices come in as that which the queen of Sheba gave King Solomon. King Solomon gave to the queen of Sheba all her desire which she requested, besides what he gave her according to his royal bounty. Then she turned and went to her own land together with her servants."

— 1 Kings 10:10, 13

The Queen of Sheba was black because Sheba was one of the sons of Cush.

"The sons of Cush were Seba and Havilah and Sabtah and Raamah and Sabteca; and the sons of Raamah were *Sheba* and Dedan."

— Genesis 10:7

What was the nature of the relationship between the Queen of Sheba and King Solomon? We can only assume that she might have gone away pregnant. Could it be that there are African descendants of this dramatic encounter between the African Queen and the Jewish king? More than likely!

Notice that after the African Queen honors the Jewish king, he gives her all that her heart desires. The *blessing* of Genesis

12:3 is put in operation for Africa! "I will bless those that bless thee."

ASSYRIA & ISRAEL'S NORTHERN KINGDOM

The Assyrian Empire harassed Israel for 100 years before finally conquering the Northern Kingdom. Northern Israel, headed by the tribe of Ephraim, (the son of Israelite Joseph with African Asnath), had gone into complete idolatry. Finally, they are all exiled to Assyria, the ruling empire of the time. The Assyrians were very cruel and separated the tribes and the families. Still today we can find vestiges of the northern tribes among the nations; in remote places such as Japan, of course in India, Bnei Menashe that recently made Alyah, (immigrated to Israel,) and Africa.

Many African tribes circumcise their sons on the 8th day after birth and they do not know why. This could be due to either some remnant of the ten northern tribes settled there or due to the connection of King Solomon with the Queen ofSheba.

Yeshua & Egypt

"Now when they had gone, behold, an angel of the Lord appeared to Joseph in a dream and said, "Get up! Take the Child and His mother and flee to Egypt, and remain there until I tell you; for Herod is going to search for the Child to destroy Him." So Joseph got up and took the Child and His mother while it was still night, and left for Egypt. He remained there until the death of Herod. This was to fulfill what had been spoken by the Lord through the prophet: "OUT OF EGYPT I CALLED MY SON."

— Matthew 2:13-15

This is the most exciting part of African-Israeli history and one that carries with it a lot of weight. The Almighty uses Egypt as a hiding place for His Messiah. Thanks to Africa, Yeshua was not killed alongside the other Jewish babies that were being slaughtered! Until it was safe in Israel, Egypt protected the child, King Yeshua. Could it be that in these end times Africa will play a major role in Israel's salvation? I believe so!

In Isaiah 19 there is an amazing promise of a three-fold relationship between Africa, Assyria, and Israel. I can see that Islam will fall in the Arab Islamic nations, such as Iraq and Iran, and in Egypt, (the Gate to Africa!,) and in all of Africa!

"Yahveh will strike Egypt, striking but healing; so they will return to Yahveh, and He will respond to them and will heal them. In that day there will be a highway from Egypt to Assyria, and the Assyrians will come into Egypt and the Egyptians into Assyria, and the Egyptians will worship with the Assyrians. In that day Israel will be the third party with Egypt and Assyria, a blessing in the midst of the earth."

— Isaiah 19:22-24

Chapter Six

THE CURE

HEALING THE RELATIONSHIP & RESTORING THE BLESSING

"Now there was a famine in the days of David for three years, year after year; and David sought the presence of the LORD. And the LORD said, "It is for Saul and his bloody house because he put the Gibeonites to death." So the king called the Gibeonites and spoke to them (now the Gibeonites were not of the sons of Israel but of the remnant of the Amorites, and the sons of Israel made a covenant with them, but Saul had sought to kill them in his zeal for the sons of Israel and Judah). Thus David said to the Gibeonites, "What should I do for you? And how can I make atonement that you may bless the inheritance of the LORD?" Then the Gibeonites said to him, "We have no concern of silver or gold with Saul or his house, nor is it for us to put any man to death in Israel." And he said, "I will do for you whatever you say."

—2 Samuel 21:1-4

I n this passage of Scripture, we can see that King David was wise; he asked the Almighty about the famine and Yahveh answered, "It is because of the sin of your predecessor, Saul" Though it was not David's fault, he assumes kingly responsibility and humbles himself before the Gibeonites. He asks forgiveness and is willing to do anything to appease them so they can bless "The inheritance

of Yahveh." David knows the wisdom of restitution.

"They buried the bones of Saul and Jonathan his son in the country of Benjamin in Zela, in the grave of Kish his father; thus they did all that the king commanded, and *after that God was moved by prayer* for the land."

— 2 Samuel 21:14

As Africa rises with the kingly wisdom of David to humble itself before Israel, ask forgiveness, and make restitution, the curse of famine will break! Israel will bless Africa and so will God!

After the Second World War, Germany was divided into East and West and there was a wall in Berlin. Though the wall fell, you can still clearly see a big difference between East and West Germany. The Russians were in East Germany and the Americans in West Germany. West Germany proceeded to ask forgiveness from the horrors committed against the Jews by the Nazi regime that exterminated six million of us in gas chambers and death pits. They also proceeded to send monetary restitution to all the survivors. Undoubtedly, Germany should have been destroyed by Elohim, but because of their repentance and practical restitution, He did not! However, East Germany on the Russian side never did that. East Germany was in terrible bondage to poverty and oppression for many years until it was united with West Germany.

It is time for Africa to renounce all political ties with the division of Israel and the establishment of a Palestinian State. No amount of "foreign aid" has been able to cure Africa! It is a lie that Africa needs to maintain "political balance" in order to survive. Africa is dying because it has given a hand to Israel's enemies and it is being judged in the Valley of Jehoshaphat.

The only politics that Africa needs is biblical politics. Biblical politics is the Key of Abraham – bless and honor Israel and you will be blessed!

The Bush Story with Biblical Politics

The following is a letter I wrote to some American Saints right after President George W. Bush was elected to the presidency of the USA.

Dear Ones:

In November of 2,000, YAHVEH the Lord sent me from Israel to Washington DC. I was scheduled to preach in Costa Rica, but had to cancel because the Holy Spirit rerouted me and told me, "Go to Washington DC." He said, "I want you to go as an Israeli to pray George W. Bush into the presidency of the USA." Well, those elections were very 'tight' and it looked like Mr. Bush needed a miracle. I obeyed God and left for Washington DC, knowing no one there.

Through a friend, I connected with the American Trust Foundation and Prayer Ministry. They received me very well, feeling the stirring of the Spirit about the reason for my coming. A lady who is the widow of a late congressman and a personal acquaintance of Mr. Bush escorted me through the two houses House of Representative and Senate and helped me to have a private showing of the White House. While at the Congress we received permission to pray at the Congressmen Chapel at "speakers corner." She said that she was experiencing more favor than usual while with me and that she had never been able to pray inside this chapel before.

There were two kneeling stools there and we both knelt on them. Then we began praying and I began declaring and prophesying Mr. Bush into the Presidency of the USA. I repeated the words God showed me, "As an Israeli, I call you to the Presidency of the United States."

Then The Lord spoke to me again as we were kneeling there, "I am calling Bush to do biblical politics in two areas:

• The internal moral affairs of the USA

• Israel

The Father kept on speaking and He said to me, "If he exercises Biblical politics in these two issues I will bless him more than any other president before him, *but if he doesn't...*"

As I listened to God I felt an awesome, sober, and very serious presence. Now election year is coming and I am concerned about the USA. President George W. Bush has been pressing Israel into having a Palestinian state. He has pushed Prime Minister Sharon into signing the infamous "road map for the division of the land." This is what Joel 3:1-3 has to say about it:

"For behold, in those days and at that time, when I bring back the captives of Judah and Jerusalem. I will also gather all nations and bring them down to the Valley of Jehoshaphat; and I will enter into judgment with them there on account of My People, My heritage Israel, whom they have scattered among the nations; they have also divided My land."

***

This letter was given to President Bush but he did not take heed and continued laboring towards the establishment of a Palestinian state.

The following is an excerpt of an article that I wrote immediately after Hurricane Katrina destroyed parts of Louisiana, Mississippi, and Alabama. The article is called: *A Rude Awakening.*

A RUDE AWAKENING

"But you have ignored all my counsel, and wanted none of my reproofs; I also will laugh at your disaster. I will mock when calamity overtakes you; when calamity over- takes you like a storm, when your disaster comes on like a whirlwind; when distress and anguish come on you. Then will they call on me, but I will not answer. They will seek me diligently, but they will not find me; because they hated knowledge, and didn't choose the fear of Yahveh."

— Proverbs 1:25-29

With an aching heart and my deepest condolences to all the bereaved and suffering in South Florida, New Orleans, Mississippi, Georgia, Romania, Switzerland, Austria, Germany, India, and all parts of the world have been victims of terrible Hurricanes, Monsoons, and Tsunami devastations. With my deepest sense of grief, and yes, even frustration for the immeasurable suffering of countless families that have lost their homes, their loved ones, and all their revenue, and yes, maybe even their hope.

With all those deep emotions and compassion for all, I write this letter. Not in order to say "I told you so", but in order to maybe provoke a world-wide wake-up call, especially in the USA. For if there will not be an awakening now, the predicaments are very terrible for the USA and for all the nations, including Great Britain, that have pushed Israel to give up precious land given by a covenant-keeping God. But if there would be an awakening, even a rude awakening, then we can expect God to "in judgment remember mercy" and have the challenging partnership between judgment and revival.

The pictures of 10,000 hard-working and devoted Jewish settlers being expelled from their homes and hothouses in Gush Katif and Northern Samaria, weeping, tearing their garments, resisting or quietly complying in brokenness, are pictures that will stay with us throughout the very hard years of history that await us. The world must remember that the Holocaust ended only 60 years ago... And that the restoration of the Jewish people to their own land, and Zionism is God's idea, and His response to the Holocaust and the endless years of violent anti-Semitism. Today is the National Funeral for all the dead from Gush Katif, whose graves are being uprooted and relocated somewhere in Israel. A solemn day indeed, not only for Israel but for the world as the following words from the mouths of the prophets resound through the ages:

"For, behold, in those days, And in that time, When I restore the fortunes of Judah and Jerusalem I will gather all nations, And will bring them down into the valley of Jehoshaphat; And I will execute judgment on them there for my people, And for my heritage, Israel, whom they have scattered among the nations. *They have divided my land.*"

— Joel 3:1-3

"For the violence done to your brother Jacob, shame will cover you, and you will be cut off forever in the day that you stood on the other side, in the day that strangers car- ried away his substance, and foreigners entered into his gates and cast lots for Jerusalem, even you were like one of them. For the day of Yahveh is near all the nations! As you have done, it will be done to you. Your deeds will return upon your own head."

— Obadiah 10-15

"I will bless those who bless you, and I will curse him who curses you. In you will all of the families of the earth be blessed."

— Genesis 12:3

***

The following is a letter that arrived to the hands of former President Bush via his Israeli Ambassador, Mr. Daniel Kurtzer, on the 14th of August, the 9th of Av, one day prior to the Gaza and Northern Samaria disengagement:

Mr. President of the USA

George W. Bush

9th of AV /14th of August 2005

Your Excellency,

The following Word was given to me by the Lord God of Abraham, Isaac, and Jacob, the God of Israel when He sent me to pray for you into the Presidency of the USA as an Israeli. I am an Israeli Jewish- Christian Bishop and regarded by many as a Prophet.

This was before you were elected to be President for the first time. The votes were being recounted in Florida. Through a series of events, I found myself at the Congressmen Chapel at Speakers Corner with Ruth Mizel the widow of late Congressman Mizel.

Ruth and I knelt on the kneeling stools and I began to pray for you and said: "As an Israeli, I call you into the Presidency of the United States."

Then the Voice of the Lord came loud and clear to me; He said:

"If George W. Bush will do *biblical politics* concerning two issues:

• The internal moral affairs of the United States.

• *Israel*

Then, he will be the *most blessed* President that the United States has *ever* had. *But if not...* (The Lord was *silent* at this point. The silence of God represents a *sure judgment*)

This is all he said.

Prior to the planned Disengagement of Gaza on the 15th of August, it is urgent that you would have this Word, as your last-minute decision will affect you and the United States in a most serious manner. If you allow the uprooting of Gush Katif and Northern Samaria, judgment will surely follow.

Respectfully yours,

Dr. Dominiquae Bierman

President of *Kad-Esh MAP Ministries*

Bishop of *TAPAC*

Jerusalem, Israel

***

Unfortunately, this prophecy came to pass just as I predicted and Hurricane Katrina, the largest catastrophe in the history of America, destroyed parts of Louisiana, Mississippi, and Alabama. People are still suffering from that catastrophe and President Bush has not learned the lesson yet and keeps pushing the "two-state solution"

The following are some of the catastrophes that have happened in the USA prior to Katrina and they are all directly related to the attempt to side with the Palestinians and divide the land of Israel.

"TEN MAJOR EVENTS RELATED TO THE U.S. & ISRAEL"

1. **October 30, 1991: The Perfect Storm** - As President George H. W. Bush is opening the Madrid (Spain) Conference to consider "land for peace" in Israel's

Middle East role, the "perfect storm" develops in the North Atlantic, creating the largest waves ever recorded in that region. The storm travels 1000 miles from "east to west" instead of the normal "west to east" pattern and crashes into the New England Coast. Thirty-five-foot waves crash into the Kennebunkport home of President Bush.

2. **August 23, 1992: Hurricane Andrew** - When the Madrid Conference moves to Washington DC and the peace talks resume, Hurricane Andrew, the worst natural disaster ever to hit America, comes ashore and produces an estimated $30 billion in damage and leaving 180,000 homeless in Florida.

3. **January 16, 1994: Northridge Earthquake** - President Bill Clinton meets with Syria's President Hafez el-Assad in Geneva. They talk about a peace agreement with Israel that includes giving up the Golan Heights. Within 24 hours, a powerful 6.9 earthquake rocks Southern California. This quake, centered in Northridge, becomes the second most destructive natural disaster to hit the United States, behind Hurricane Andrew.

4. **January 21, 1998: Lewinsky Scandal** - Israeli Prime Minister Benjamin Netanyahu meets with President Clinton at the White House and is coldly received. Clinton and Secretary of State Madeleine Albright refuse to have lunch with him. Shortly afterward on that day, the Monica

Lewinsky scandal breaks into the mass media and begins to occupy a major portion of Clinton's time.

5. **September 28, 1998: Hurricane George** - As Secretary of State Albright works on the final details of an agreement in which Israel would give up 13 percent of Yesha (Judah and Samaria), Hurricane George slams into the United States Gulf Coast with 110 mph winds and gusts up to 175 mph. The hurricane hits the coast and stalled. On September 28, Clinton meets with Yasser Arafat and Netanyahu at the White House to finalize this land deal. Later, Arafat addresses the United Nations about declaring an independent Palestinian state by May 1999, as Hurricane George pounds the Gulf Coast, causing $1 billion in damage. At the exact time that Arafat departs the country, the storm begins to dissipate.

6. 6 October 15-22, 1998: Texas Flooded - On October 15, 1998, Arafat and Netanyahu meet at the Wye River Plantation in Maryland. The talks are scheduled to last five days with the focus on Israel giving up 13 percent of Yesha. The talks are extended and conclude on October 23. On October 17, awesome rains and tornadoes hit southern Texas. The San Antonio area is deluged with rain. The rain and flooding in Texas continue until October 22 and then subside. The floods ravage 25 percent of Texas and leave over one billion dollars in

damage. On October 21, Clinton declares this section of Texas a major disaster area.

7. **November 30, 1998: Market Capitalization Evaporates** – Arafat comes to Washington again to meet with President Clinton to raise money for a Palestinian state with Jerusalem as the capital. A total of 42 other nations were represented in Washington. All the nations agreed to give Arafat $3 billion in aid. Clinton promised

8. $400 million, and the European nations $1.7 billion. On the same day, the Dow Jones average drops 216 points, and on December 1, the European Market had its third worst day in history. Hundreds of billions of market capitalization were wiped out in the U.S. and Europe.

9. **December 12, 1998: Clinton is Impeached** - As Clinton lands in the Palestinian-controlled section of Israel to discuss the "land for peace" process, the House of Representatives votes four articles of impeachment against him.

10. **May 3, 1999: The Powerful Super Tornado** - On the day that Yasser Arafat is scheduled to declare a Palestinian state with Jerusalem as the capital, the most powerful tornado storm system ever to hit the United States sweeps across Oklahoma and Kansas. The winds are clocked at 316 mph the fastest wind speed ever

recorded. The declaration is postponed to December 1999 at the request of President Clinton, whose letter to Arafat encourages him in his "aspirations for his land." He also writes that the Palestinians have a right to "determine their future on their own land" and that they deserve to "live free, today, tomorrow and forever."

11. **Week of October 11, 2000: Hurricane, Earthquake, and Dow Collapse** - As Jewish settlers in 15 West Bank (Israel) settlements are evicted from the covenant land in Israel, the Dow- Jones financial averages lose 5.7 percent in the worst week since October 1989. On October 15 the Dow lost 266 points, and a hurricane slams into North Carolina. On the next morning, October 16, a magnitude 7.1 earthquake rocks the southwest in the fifth most powerful earthquake in the 20th Century. The earthquake was centered in the California desert and did little damage but was felt in three states.*

In John McTernan's book, *Israel: The Blessing or the Curse*, and Bill Koenig's *Eye to Eye* as mentioned in my book, *Stormy Weather,* we identify events that occur on the same day that Israel was strongly advised, or forced, to give up her covenant land by the United States or others. The above gives one an idea of the magnitude of these events.

---

* Koenig's International News: watch-news@watch.org, 6/12/02. URL: http://www.watch.org

What About Africa?

In his book about Israel and Africa, Joel Peters writes,

> "The resolutions on the Middle East conflict adopted by the meetings of the OAU after 1973 *expressed full support for the Arabs.* At the 1974 OAU summit in Mogadishu, Somalia, the African states listed a number of conditions for the attainment of a just and lasting peace in the Middle East. These were:

12. The complete withdrawal of Israel from all the occupied territories (notice that this is part of the covenant land – Dominiquae Bierman) to the lines of June 4, 1967

13. The liberation of the Arab city of Jerusalem (the eternal capital of Israel! – Dominiquae Bierman)

14. The exercise by the Palestinian people of the right to self-determination and the implementation of the resolutions of the United Nations relating to the Palestine question.

Missing from this list was any guarantee of the sovereignty, territorial integrity, and political independence of Israel. Furthermore, the African states no longer included any direct references to UN resolution 242. The OAU also confirmed at that meeting, for the first time, its total support for the Palestinian Liberation Organization as the sole representative of the Palestinian people and called upon its members to aid the organization in its just national struggle. The tones of the resolutions adopted by the OAU

55

became unreservedly hostile towards Israel. The African states denounced Zionism as a danger to world peace."*

Is it, therefore, a surprise that Africa is in such a condition of poverty, disease, and humiliation? The moment that Africa repents, makes restitution, reciprocates, and establishes clear biblical relationship with Israel, it will be blessed by Yahveh and by all of Israel's expertise. Contrary to other foreigners that came to colonize, subdue and exploit Africa, Israel has always sought to help Africa in every arena possible. The response by Africa of supporting the Palestinians has caused the *curse* to come upon Africa. Israel has been sold to her enemies, terror has escalated, Iran wants to annihilate her, and she is suffering. The mother of all nations has been sold to her enemies by her own friends and children; let us remember that half of Africa is Christian! The Word of God says, "Whoever repays evil for good, evil will never leave his house" Africa has repaid Israel "evil for *good.*" In order to stop the plague, Africa must repent and make restitution! Together with King David, Africa should say, "What must I do so that you (Israel) will bless the inheritance of Yahveh (Africa)."

THE CHURCH LEVEL

Repentance and restitution must be sought first at the church level. The church in a nation is the priest of that nation, and most especially in Africa, where recent statistics say that almost 50% of all Africans are Christians of some persuasion. Because

* Joel Peters, *Israel, and Africa: the Problematic Friendship* pgs. 72, 73

of the large percentage of Christians in Africa, Africa's betrayal of Israel is even more serious.

"For it is time for judgment to begin with the household of God; and if it begins with us first, what will be the outcome for those who do not obey the gospel of God? AND IF IT IS WITH DIFFICULTY THAT THE RIGHTEOUS IS SAVED, WHAT WILL BECOME OF THE GODLESS MAN AND THE SINNER?"

— 1 Peter 4:17-18

A few years ago, I visited the death camps of Auschwitz in Poland for the first time. I was so shocked by what I saw there and was particularly shaken when I saw that there were churches all around that would have seen the smoke of the cremated bodies of my Jewish people coming out of the chimneys! I asked the Father, *How could this (catastrophe) have been prevented?"*

His answer was, "There was no 'Esther church' at that time."

Queen Esther was willing to risk her life to intercede spiritually before God and physically before the Persian King for her people! But why didn't the church at that time identify itself with Israel? I saw a picture in an exhibition in Auschwitz and it showed all the Christian leaders, evangelicals included, giving to Hitler the "right hand of fellowship." While there were isolated cases of goodness from the side of Christians toward the suffering Jews, no Christian organization rose to oppose Hitler's regime; however, most of Germany was Protestant and most of Poland was Catholic. Christians were passive at best and many actively helped Hitler! How can something like this be? The answer is simple; the church did not identify itself with Israel because it was totally divorced from its real identity as being grafted into the Olive Tree (read Romans 11). In fact, it was and still is steeped in replacement theology, a deathly theology that was institutionalized with Christianity by Emperor Constantine through the Council of Nicaea. replacement theology has been the villain behind all Christian anti-Semitism! It was established as church doctrine with the act of discarding the Jewish Shabbat and exchanging it for Sunday because Emperor Constantine was a sun worshipper. It proceeded to discard the biblical Passover for Easter, a celebration derived from the pagan goddess of fertility, Ishtar, and it discarded the whole Hebrew Scriptures as old and obsolete renaming them "Old Testament." It also called for the complete separation between Gentile Christians and all Jews. (See appendix at the end of this book.)

Eventually, it sanctioned and encouraged persecution and public humiliation of Jews because "They killed Christ." It is important to note that though the religious, Jewish leaders handed the Messiah over to the Romans, they could not exercise the death penalty, so actually, the Messiah was crucified by Romans. The real issue is that Yeshua laid down His life for the salvation of all. Without His shed blood, there is no forgiveness of sins! Replacement theology in all its aspects has placed the Gentile Christians in a very precarious situation.

"But if some of the branches were broken off, and you, being a wild olive, were grafted in among them and became partaker with them of the rich root of the olive tree, do not be arrogant toward the branches; but if you are arrogant, remember that it is not you who supports the root, but the root supports you.*

You will say then, "Branches were broken off so that I might be grafted in." Quite right, they were broken off for their unbelief, but you stand by your faith. Do not be conceited, but fear; for if God did not spare the natural branches, He will not spare you, either. Behold then the kindness and severity of God; to those who fell, severity, but to you, God's kindness, if you continue in His kindness; otherwise you also will be cut off."

— Romans 11:17-22

The church in Africa has inherited replacement theology and Christian anti-Semitism from the European version of Christianity. Europe inherited it from Constantine and the 4th century church fathers. The only hope to get rid of this theology, that has brought death to the Jews and curses to the nations, is by renouncing it all together, and by reconnecting again with Israel, with the Jewish roots of the faith, and with the original Gospel "made in Zion."

Since the Jubilee of Israel in 1998, the heavenly shofar (trumpet) has been sounding. It is calling the church to repent from replacement theology, anti-Semitism, pagan feasts, and celebrations inherited through Constantine and the Council of Nicaea, and to return to the original Jewish foundations of faith. I strongly suggest that you order *the MAP Revolution* series on this subject, beginning with the book *The Healing Power of the Roots* and *Grafted In*. (See the list in the appendix of this book)

As the church in Africa repents from replacement theology and gets grafted into the Olive Tree with Israel, it will have the anointing "to repent" and "to make restitution" on behalf of

59

their respective nations. Any church leadership that will choose to take this course of action will be thoroughly blessed and will catapult its nation out of the curse.

Please turn immediately to the Appendixes at the end of the book before you continue reading.

Practical Steps to Take

1. Individual and corporate renouncing of the Council of Nicaea and replacement theology (see Appendix at the end of the book).

2. Prayer of repentance for the sins of commission and omission of your nation concerning Israel

3. Financial restitution to Israel. Before you take this step please contact our ministry so it can be coordinated properly and it can reach the right channels.

4. Pray for Israel first and the peace of Jerusalem. Most people pray for revival in their nation first. But if you pray for Israel first according to God's word, you will then have the favor to pray for your nation and will see results. (Psalms 122:6, 137:5-6 and Romans 1:16)

5. Proceed to cleanse the church or ministry under your care from the effects of replacement theology . Call us to coordinate a "Healing Power of the Roots" seminar so you and your people can be taught the Gospel in its original Jewish context. This will restore Holy Worship and morality and will change the face of the African Society. This is the true fulfillment of the Great Commission – to teach Yahveh's Commandments to the nations. Yeshua said in Matthew 28:19,20: *"Go therefore and make disciples of all nations...**teaching them to obey all***

that I commanded you; and lo, I am with you always, even to the end of the age." This He spoke to His Jewish disciples and apostles and now at the end of the age, Jewish apostles are rising up again to teach God's Commandments to the nations!

6. Making "Spiritual Alyah;" come up to Zion. The Word of God promises great blessings to those that come up to bless Israel and to bless the Name of Yahveh in Zion. (Isaiah 2:1-3, 2 Chronicles 6:34, Zechariah 8:21-23). Your presence in the land of Israel when you come to pray, tour, and learn in the land has a tremendous impact on the Spirit.

"The word which Isaiah the son of Amoz saw concerning Judah and Jerusalem: Now it will come about that In the last days The mountain of the house of the LORD will be established as the chief of the mountains, And will be raised above the hills; And all the nations will stream to it. And many peoples will come and say, "Come, let us go up to the mountain of the LORD, To the house of the God of Jacob, That He may teach us concerning His ways And that we may walk in His paths. "For the law will go forth from Zion, and the Word of the LORD from Jerusalem."

— Isaiah 2:1-3

7. Actively in prayer, support, speech, finances, stand for the rights of the people of Israel to their land and for their Alyah, (return to Zion,) from all the nations of the earth. **Do not agree with those that advocate the**

establishment of a Palestinian state or removal of Jewish settlements in biblical lands; remember they are "God's enemies!" (Psalm 83)

8. Promote the message in this book so that all of Africa can come out of the curse and into the Blessing!

THE GOVERNMENT LEVEL

Once you have proceeded with the above steps, it is time to speak to your government and challenge it to repent towards Israel and to change its policies. This needs to be a public act accompanied by a renewal of political ties and the establishing of your African Embassy in Jerusalem. All the embassies of the nations are now in Tel Aviv refusing to recognize Jerusalem as the capital of Israel. This is an act of dishonor; therefore, it incurs in the Genesis 12:3 Meera-curse, because of Klala-dishonoring or taking Israel lightly! This one act of public repentance, restitution, and the establishing of the African Embassies in Jerusalem rather than Tel Aviv, has the power to overturn the situation in Africa. Some believers in Messiah that will apply the principles presented in this book will rise to prominence in government in their nations.

"But Judah will be inhabited forever And Jerusalem for all generations. And I will avenge their blood which I have not avenged, For the LORD dwells in Zion."

— Joel 3:20,21

Remember that we should refrain from blaming the government, but rather take responsibility for the situation and the sins of Africa. Adam relinquished his responsibility when he blamed his wife rather than face Elohim in repentance. What happened next was that the Creator banished both of them out of the Garden. Had Adam taken his leadership role in repenting for the sin, I believe that man would still be in the Garden of Eden (Genesis 3:10-24). Poverty, sickness, and disease have affected all of Africa, Christians included, but the true believers in Messiah have the power to get their nation out from darkness into the light if you follow the simple steps presented in this book.

The black (Cushite) prophet Zephaniah predicted something that would happen at the end of the age:

"Therefore wait for Me," declares the LORD, "For the day when I rise up as a witness, indeed, My decision is to gather nations, to assemble kingdoms, to pour out on them My indignation, all My burning anger; for all the earth will be devoured by the fire of My zeal. "For then I will give to the peoples purified lips, that all of them may call on the name of Yahveh, to serve Him shoulder to shoulder. *"From beyond the rivers of Ethiopia My worshipers, My dispersed ones, will bring My offerings.* "In that day you will feel no shame because of all your deeds by which you have rebelled against Me; for then I will remove from your midst your proud, exulting ones, and you will never again be haughty on My holy mountain."

— Zephaniah 3:8-11

These worshippers from beyond the rivers of Ethiopia are the African believers coming to Zion and bringing offerings. This act of worship, and restitution towards Israel, and the God of Israel, will permanently remove the shame, the poverty, and the disease of Africa! I also believe that when Israel sees the genuineness of this repentance, it will again be released to assist Africa through agriculture, construction, and other technical abilities.

I know of a wonderful African believer in Burkina Faso that began to apply these principles with a small sacrificial offering towards a Messianic congregation in Israel. Slowly he increased the offering coming from his very poor people and he arrived in Israel one day with thousands of dollars that he put in the hands of the Messianic Israeli pastor. Today the government of Israel is helping his people in Burkina Faso to establish high-tech agriculture, which is on the way to remove famine from Burkina Faso. This precious African brother understood the Key of Abraham of Genesis 12:3 and applied it to his people and nation. He began with what he could and did not delegate the responsibility to others bigger than himself. Elohim is not bound to save by many or by few and He is no respecter of persons.

"There will be tribulation and distress for every soul of man who does evil, of the Jew first and also of the Greek, but glory and honor and peace to everyone who does good, to the Jew first and also to the Greek, for there is no partiality with God."

— Romans 2:9-11

Closure

END WORD

As all the nations of the earth turn against Israel and force her to give up her Biblical land as well as vow to annihilate her, may the continent of Africa arise as a protector of Israel, making restitution for past sins. As Africa applies this Bible Cure it will come out of immorality, poverty, and disease and take its place among the world superpowers as an end-time leader, leading the rest of the nations into the same repentance.

In the book of Matthew, Yeshua separates the sheep and the goat nations according to how they treated "The least of his brethren" (the Jews!) in the time of their need. All nations closed the doors before the Jewish refugees of the Nazi Holocaust, now again threats of destruction are coming against Israel! May all of Africa become a "sheep continent" by rising to the occasion and defending Israel.

"All the nations will be gathered before Him; and He will separate them from one another, as the shepherd separates the sheep from the goats; and He will put the sheep on His right,

and the goats on the left. "Then the King will say to those on His right, 'Come, you who are blessed of My Father, inherit the kingdom prepared for you from the foundation of the world. 'For I was hungry, and you gave Me something to eat; I was thirsty, and you gave Me something to drink; I was a stranger, and you invited Me in; naked, and you clothed Me; I was sick, and you visited Me; I was in prison, and you came to Me.' "Then the righteous will answer Him, 'Lord, when did we see You hungry, and feed You, or thirsty, and give You something to drink? 'And when did we see You a stranger, and invite You in, or naked, and clothe You? 'When did we see You sick, or in prison, and come to You?' "The King will answer and say to them, 'Truly I say to you, *to the extent that you did it to one of these brothers of Mine, even the least of them, you did it to Me.*'

— Matthew 25:32-40

The natural brothers of Yeshua are the Jewish people!

As you seek to apply THE BIBLE CURE for Africa, we, as a ministry, are ready to assist you in taking the official steps of repentance and restitution. Not long ago I was invited by a Malaysian woman to come and teach a conference on the Holy Feast of Passover. Malaysia is a Moslem country, an enemy of Israel, and I could not even go in as an Israeli. I tried to evade my coming because it was my Sabbatical Year, (after 17 years of concentrated ministry!) but this precious lady minister wrote me a desperate letter saying,

"Yeshua told me that if you do not come, my country is going to be lost."

Her tone of voice was so desperate that compassion rose within me and I went. As pastors and leaders in the conference were making an act of repentance of the sins of Malaysia towards Israel, they went on their knees and asked my forgiveness as a Jew, an Israeli Bishop, and representative of my people. As I extended forgiveness and broke the curse, there was a great anointing and a great peace. This had been the first time that the flag of Israel had been raised on stage publicly in Malaysia. Immediately, as we left the conference hall, some news arrived: the Ringgit, the Malaysian currency, had just gone up for the first time in nine years since the government of Malaysia had spoken openly against Israel. Not only that, but it was the highest rate recorded in the history of Malaysia! Later on, I also heard some news of political change concerning the restrictions of Islam on Christians.

At the same time that this news was coming in April of 2007, some other news from Africa came in by SMS message into the cell phone. President Gbagbo, of Ivory Coast, was signing a miraculous treaty between the north and the south thus ending years of devastating civil war. I had been with my team in Ivory Coast invited by Bishop Amazou of TAPAC and some prayers of repentance against replacement theology were made. Also through Bishop Amazou's coordination, we were received in the Presidential Palace by the First Lady. However, the favor of Yahveh was upon us and we were invited three more times. One of the times I had the privilege of preaching during the Christmas service to President Gbagbo and his guests who received my message on Israel enthusiastically. Their reception and their welcome to this Jew with this message of repentance released the favor and the blessing to Ivory Coast, so peace came and with peace comes also healing and prosperity.

"For if their (the Jews) rejection is the reconciliation of the world, what will their (the Jews) acceptance be but life from the dead?"

— Romans 11:15

My prayer is that Ivory Coast, and the church there, will keep on humbling themselves before Elohim towards Israel and learning of the Jewish roots of the faith so that it can be established as a sheep nation. And that many more African nations will follow quickly before time is too late!

"For behold, the day is coming, burning like a furnace, and all the arrogant and every evildoer will be chaff, and the day that is coming will set them ablaze," says the LORD of hosts, "so that it will leave them neither root nor branch." *"But for you who fear My name, the sun of righteousness will rise with healing in its wings; and you will go forth and skip about like calves from the stall."*

— Malachi 4:1,2

With love in Yeshua,
Archbishop Dr. Dominiquae Bierman
Jerusalem, Israel

Appendix 1

TWO WEDDINGS & ONE DIVORCE

THE FIRST MARRIAGE

The following illustration will explain why Christianity was 'the womb' of the Spanish Inquisition, the Crusades, and the Nazi Holocaust. Yahveh-God is looking to the church for repentance in order to influence the nations and fulfill the mandate of Matthew 28:19 *"Go and make disciples of all nations."*

The first and original church was married to a Jewish Husband by the name of Yeshua the Messiah & into His family the Jewish people (Ephesians 2:14 and Romans 11). The Wedding Ceremony took place in Jerusalem. It was ratified and sealed by the spilling of the blood of the Husband and by the breaking of His body. (Luke 22:15–20) The time of this marriage was the holy biblical Feast of Passover. The fruit of this miraculous wedding was thousands and thousands of people, both Jews and Gentiles, saved and healed. Even the shadow of this holy bride healed the sick, as signs and wonders and miracles followed her wherever she went in the name of her Husband Yeshua.

This marriage led the wife to much suffering. Many in the world did not love her Husband and tried to kill her by persecuting her and even throwing her to the lions during the Roman Empire's reign of terror. Those were hard years. After many years of suffering, Yeshua's wife had become weary. He had gone to prepare a place for her and had not come back yet.

She started to get tired from her lifestyle as an outcast, persecuted and hunted at every corner. She longed for peace at any price. She longed for the warm embrace of a Husband who would provide her with peace and security here on this earth... At her weakest point an earthly king appeared. (Matthew 10:34, John 14:27, Jeremiah 8:11)

This earthly king was influential and powerful by earthly standards. He could stop the killing and persecution against her. He could give her the security she longed for... *If* only she would agree to divorce this Jewish Husband of hers and completely separate from His family Israel, and from that Book that she treasured so much – where He had left her all of His instructions and the family legacy of God's Word.

This powerful king seemed to be a spiritual man. He claimed that her Jewish Husband had appeared to him in a dream and had given him the crown of the Roman Empire. His deceptive charm and appeasing manners managed to attract the very weary bride of Messiah, but not all were deceived. There was a portion of the bride/church/ecclesia that was not fooled by the charms of this deceitful king. These were the Messianic Jews of the time.

They were too rooted in the writings of the Holy Book and the ancient Hebrew Scriptures to be deceived. But the vast majority of the believers at that time were Gentiles, and they did not want any more suffering on behalf of the Book, its Author, or His family.

They wanted freedom and peace at all cost.

The powerful Constantine sang the song of peace and safety and prepared a bed of roses... The Gentile portion of the church slept with him, falling into violent adultery and wounding the heart of her heavenly Jewish Husband. In order to appease the conscience of this adulterous church, Constantine decided to legalize this unholy union in the year AD 325 by means of a wedding ceremony called the Council of Nicaea and drawing up an ungodly and illegal marriage contract called the Nicean Creed.

He used his worldly power to draw all the gentile church fathers, which for the most part were already anti-Semitic and hated their Jewish roots. These church fathers were to be witnesses of this horrendous divorce and the adulterous new marriage between the predominantly Gentile church and another Jesus, a product of Constantine's own creation.

This alternative Savior came with another family, another book (totally disconnected from the ancient Hebrew writings), other customs, Laws, festivals, traditions and ways of measuring time.

Knowing that his brand-new wife was accustomed to worshipping God, he organized for her a god that would suit her perfectly by not demanding any holiness from her. He presented a god of peace that was lenient towards a mixture of paganism and holiness: An all-inclusive god, who accepted all traditions and blended them into one.

Now Passover and First Fruits, the festival of Yeshua's resurrection, would become The Feast of Ishtar, the goddess of fertility, or Easter with bunny rabbits and Easter eggs. (At that time eggs were dipped in the blood of the babies sacrificed to the goddess, thus the tradition of painting the eggs).

Now the fay of worship would change from Shabbat to Sunday in order to eternalize the sun god who for now would be called Jesus – yet it was another Jesus and certainly not Yeshua, the Jewish Messiah.

Then the day of the winter solstice of witchcraft, called Saturnalia or Paganalia, celebrated on the 25th of December in the Roman Empire, was to acquire the name Christmas and would celebrate the birth of this false Messiah. For the true Messiah was born during the holy biblical Feast of Tabernacles and followed the Hebrew biblical calendar, not the Roman one. (Daniel 7:25–27, Jeremiah 10:2–4 about the Christmas tree.)

The ancient Holy Book of the Hebrew Scriptures was to become obsolete, and its Laws done away with. Instead, Constantine compiled the apostolic writings, the letters of Paul and others into a new holy book and called it the New Testament. He gave this holy book his own perverse interpretation, completely divorced from the foundational Hebrew Writings whom he and his followers called the 'Old Testament.' (Matthew 5:17–21)

"In rejecting their custom, we may transmit to our descendants the legitimate way of celebrating Easter... We ought not therefore to have anything in common with the Jew, for the Savior has shown us another way; our worship following a more legitimate and more convenient course (the order of the days of the week); And consequently, in unanimously adopting this mode, we desire dearest brethren to separate ourselves from the detestable company of the Jew." (Excerpt from *The Nicene Creed*, year 325, found in *Eusebius, Vita Const. Lib III 18-20)*

This creed and its instructions are still followed by most Christians today with the celebration of Easter, Christmas, Sunday (replacing Shabbat), and the rejection of the Laws of God.

Indeed, a new religion had been born. It had a gentile god by the name of Jesus Christ, an apostle by the name of Constantine, a new book by the name of the New Testament (although compiled from the apostolic writings, which are completely Yah-inspired, it was deceitfully interpreted through gentile eyes and gentile theologians), and new traditions, and unholy festivals such as Easter, Christmas, Sunday, and Halloween.

And most importantly... *no Jews*... no, not even the Messiah.

What has been the fruit of this adulterous marriage?

Either make the tree good and its fruit good, or else make the tree bad and its fruit bad; for a tree is known by its fruit.

Matthew 12:33

The fruit of the first holy matrimony were salvations and healings. The fruit of this ungodly and pagan marriage were forced conversions and killings, yes even mass destructions of the family of Yeshua the Messiah, (the true Husband), in the name of the false Jesus Christ god created by Constantine.

A god who, according to Constantine in the Nicene Creed, had shown us *another way*. What was that way? It is a way of jealousy, hatred, killing, destruction, and Lawlessness. Horrendous Christian events such as pogroms, the holy inquisition, and the holocaust, have taken place since this ungodly 4th century marriage and the creation of this false religion.

The hatred conveyed in the Nicene Creed against the Jews and anything Jewish, including the Torah and the Old Testament, has continued through the great Protestant Reformation of the 16th century, and it still influences Christians today.

The following excerpt is from *Our Hands are Stained with Blood* by Michael Brown, as he quotes directly from Martin Luther's writings.

Luther wrote this after he was frustrated from trying to evangelize the Jews and when he was old and sick:

"What shall we Christians do with this damned rejected race of Jews? First, their synagogues should be set on fire. Secondly, their homes should likewise be broken down and destroyed. Thirdly, they should be deprived of their prayer books and Talmud's. Fourthly, their rabbis must be forbidden under threat of death to teach anymore. Fifthly, passports and traveling privileges should be absolutely forbidden to the Jews... To sum up dear princes and nobles, who have Jews in your domains, if this advice of mine does not suit you, then find a better one. So that you and we may all be free of this insufferable, devilish burden – the Jews." (Luther and Brown)

Hitler followed Luther's instructions meticulously and quoted him while doing so. The fruit? Over six million Jews exterminated in horrendous death camps and gas chambers, and many survivors scarred for life.

PROPHETIC ALTAR CALL

After two days He will revive us; on the third day He will raise us up, that we may live in His sight. Let us know; let us pursue the knowledge of Yahveh. His going forth is established as the morning; He will come to us like the rain, like the latter and former rain to the earth.

Hosea 6:2–3

The Third Day is upon us, the Third Millennium, and this is the Father's call to His Third Day church:

Come let us return to Yeshua, to our Jewish Messiah, His Jewish family and His ancient Hebrew Scriptures. Come let us reinterpret the New Testament through the eyes of the holy Scriptures. Let us separate ourselves from our pagan husband, Constantine, and his false Jesus and let us go back to the true Messiah Yeshua, to His Father's Laws and Precepts, to true divine holy grace, to true love and holiness. Let us return to Jerusalem, and let us be made whole from centuries of adultery and paganism, as we go back to the original apostolic Jewish roots of our faith.

In Yeshua's love and brokenness;
Archbishop Dr. Dominiquae & Rabbi Baruch Bierman

Disclaimer: What this Article is Not Saying

- It is *not* saying to go back to the laws of Rabbinic Judaism.

- It is *not* implying that all Christians have anti-Semitism.

- It is *not* disqualifying the countless believers who call on the name of Jesus Christ meaning the *true* Jewish Messiah Yeshua.

- It is *not* disqualifying worship on Sunday, Monday, Tuesday or any other day.

- It is *not* disqualifying the New Testament as Bible (Only the wrong, 'divorced' interpretations of it).

REVOCATION OF THE COUNCIL OF NICAEA

From the letter of the Emperor (Constantine) to all those not present at the council. (Found in Eusebius, Vita Const., Lib III 18-20)

When the question relative to the sacred festival of Easter arose, it was universally thought that it would be convenient that all should keep the feast on one day; for what could be more beautiful and more desirable than to see this festival, through which we receive the hope of immortality, celebrated by all with one accord and in the same manner? It was declared to be particularly unworthy for this, the holiest of festivals, to follow the customs (the calculation) of the Jews who had soiled their hands with the most fearful of crimes, and whose minds were blinded. In rejecting their custom we may transmit to our descendants the legitimate mode of celebrating Easter; which we have observed from the time of the Saviour's passion (according to the day of the week).

We ought not, therefore, to have anything in common with the Jew, for the Saviour has shown us another way; our worship following a more legitimate and more convenient course (the order of the days of the week: And consequently in unanimously adopting this mode, we desire, dearest brethren to separate ourselves from the detestable company of the Jew. For it is truly shameful for us to hear them boast that without their direction, we could not keep this feast. How can they be in the right, they who, after the death of the Saviour, have no longer been led by reason but by wild violence, as their delusion may urge them? They do not possess the truth in this Easter question, for in their blindness and repugnance to all improvements they frequently celebrate two Passovers in the same year. We could not imitate those who are openly in error.

How, then, could we follow these Jews who are most certainly blinded by error? For to celebrate a Passover twice in one year, is totally inadmissible.

But even if this were not so it would still be your duty not to tarnish your soul by communication with such wicked people (the Jews). You should consider not only that the number of churches in these provinces make a majority, but also that it is right to demand what our reason approves, and that we should have nothing in common with the Jews. (Gleaned from Dr. Henry R. Percival's *"The Nicaean and Post Nicaean Fathers."* Vol. XIV Grand Rapid: Erdmans pub. 1979, pgs. 54-55)

EXPOSING THE 23 LIES & DOCTRINAL ERRORS

1. "When the question relative to the sacred festival of Easter..."

The truth: sacred to pagan traditions, this is a pagan name derived from the goddess Ishtar. (Exodus 20:3, Hosea 2:17)

2. "...arose, it was universally..."

The truth: Everyone in the universe? Is Constantine the king of the universe? (Isaiah 14:3)

3. "...thought that it would be convenient..."

The truth: God does not call us to convenience but obedience. (John 15:10)

4. "...that all should keep the feast on one day; for what could be more beautiful and more desirable than to see this festival, through which we receive the hope of immortality, celebrated by all with one accord and in the same manner?...."

The truth: Without Jews? John 17:21, unity between Jew and Gentile brings the salvation of all mankind. (Psalms 133 and Isaiah 56)

5. "...It was declared to be particularly unworthy..."

The truth: Yahveh's choice of dates is "unworthy" to Constantine as he sets himself above God's choosing of timings. (Daniel 7:25 and Isaiah 14:13 [Lucifer])

6. "...for this, the holiest of festivals to follow the customs (the calculation) of the Jews..."

The truth: Which are the original and true calculations? (Leviticus 23:1, Jeremiah 31:31–34)

7. "...who had soiled their hands with the most fearful of crimes, and whose minds were blinded..."

The truth: In John 10:17–18 Yeshua lays His own life down (See also John 3:16.) the accusation that "The Jews killed Christ" has been the incentive for the extermination of millions of Jews from that point onwards and until this day, including the Holocaust. (See Matthew 7:17–20, the fruit of this theology)

8. "...In rejecting their custom..."

The truth: God's custom according to His Word.

9. "...we may transmit to our descendants the legitimate..."

The truth: according to Constantine but not according to the Word of God. (Matthew 26:2, Leviticus 23:1–4, Genesis 1:14, John 20:1–9, Matthew 12:39)

10. "...mode of celebrating Easter which we have observed..."

The truth: pagan name and feast not mentioned in the Holy Scriptures.

11. "We ought not therefore to have anything in common with the Jew, for the Savior has shown us another way"

The truth: Yeshua is Jewish, so if nothing is in common with the Jews, nothing is in common with the Messiah. (Matthew 1, John 19;19, Luke 1:59, Luke 2:21)

12. "our worship following a more legitimate and more convenient course, the order of the days of the week"

The truth: Constantine legitimizes his own ideas in order to gain political power and control and he attempts to dethrone the Word of God on this subject – setting himself and his opinions above Yah and His unchanging Word.

13. "...And consequently in unanimously..."

The truth: without the Jews from which salvation comes! (John 4:22)

14. "...adopting this mode, we desire, dearest brethren to separate ourselves from the detestable company of the Jew For it is truly shameful for us to hear them boast that without their direction we could not keep this feast. How can they be in the right, they who, after the death of the Savior..."

The truth: Romans 11:15–20 warns the Gentiles not to be arrogant against the Jews or Gentiles will be cut of the Olive tree!

15. "...have no longer been led by reason..."

The truth: True sons of God are not led by reason or Greek philosophy but by the Spirit of God. Since Constantine and the Council of Nicaea, the church in its vast majority has been led by reason and by theologians instead of by powerful apostles. (Romans 8:14, Ephesians 2:20) – these are all Jewish.

16. "but by wild violence, as their delusion may urge them"

The truth: What wild violence is he talking about? Unsupported accusation used many times to incite the masses against the Jews like in the Protocols of the Elders of Zion?

17. "They do not possess the truth in this Easter question, for in their blindness and [15th lie] repugnance to all improvements"

The truth: traditions of demons and men that make null and void the Word of God (Matthew 15:3,4, Mark 7:13)

18. "They frequently celebrate two Passovers in the same year.

We could not imitate those who are openly in error. How, then, could we follow these Jews who are most certainly blinded by error?"

The truth: Is following the biblical customs error? Who is really blinded here? Gentiles are supposed to be grafted into Israel's Olive tree and not vice versa! (Romans 11:15–20)

19. "For to celebrate a Passover twice in one year is totally inadmissible."

    The truth: 2 Chronicles 30:1–3, it is totally scriptural.

20. "But even if this were not so it would still be your duty not to tarnish your soul by communication with such wicked people (the Jews)."

    The truth: In other words, Constantine's purpose is to separate from the Jews and the Torah no matter what! Why? 1 John 4:1–3 states that the spirit of anti-Messiah, in operation through Constantine, removes the identity of Messiah as a Jew, and sets himself above God and His Word and His sovereign choice of choosing the Jews to bring salvation.

21. "You should consider not only that the number of churches in these provinces make a majority"

    The truth: God has never worked with "majorities" but with obedience. Trusting in the arm of the flesh or the opinions of men brings about a curse! (Deuteronomy 28:1–14, Jeremiah 17:5, Judges 7:2–8, 1 Samuel 14:6)

22. "...but also that it is right to demand what our reason approves..."

The truth: Human reasoning? (1 Corinthians 1:27, Isaiah 29:14b)

23. "...and that we should have nothing in common with the Jews."

The truth: or with the Jewish Messiah or His salvation – John 4:22, Romans 11:15–20. He set the Gentile part of the church onto a path of self-destruction, remaining a wild olive instead of being grafted into the cultivated Olive tree – which is Israel – because of arrogance, removing the foundations of the Jewish apostles and prophets. (Psalms 11:3, Ephesians 2:20, Revelation 21:14)

PRAYER RENOUNCING THE FIRST COUNCIL OF NICAEA

Please pray. You can copy and pass it on, and please let us know of your decision.

Before the Almighty God of Israel, I stand and hereby renounce the First Council of Nicaea as led by Constantine. I renounce its foundation and all the anti-Jewish fruit that came out of it. I renounce every doctrinal error and every lie in it, including replacement theology in all of its aspects.

I hereby affirm my faith in Yahveh, the God of Israel, who is the Creator of the Universe and my Father through the atoning death of His Holy Son Yeshua, who is both the promised Jewish Messiah and God in the flesh. I hereby affirm my faith in the resurrection of Yeshua the Messiah and the outpouring of the Holy Spirit of God from the Day of Shavuot (Pentecost) and onwards, to all that repent and believe in the Son. I hereby affirm my belief that I am grafted into the Olive Tree that represents Israel, and together with the believing Jewish people, I will inherit eternal life. I hereby affirm that the God of Israel will never forsake His people, neither will He forget His covenant with the Jews or with the Ecclesia (Called out Ones - Church).

I thank You, Holy Father, for removing all the curses that have come into my life and into my nation due to our belief in the tenets of faith stated in the Council of Nicaea concerning the Jews and the Jewish foundations of the faith. I beg You and thank You for pouring out Your great mercy and forgiveness over myself, my family, and my nation. I hereby commit myself to walk in truth as You reveal it to me and in love with all my fellow men and especially my (and the Church's) spiritual parents, the Jewish people, according to Genesis 12:1-3.

Appendix 3

CONNECT WITH US

Visit our websites & follow us in social media

United Nations for Israel

Take a stand for the restoration of Israel and transform your
nation into a Sheep Nation, one person at a time.
Become a member and join our monthly online conferences to
get equipped!
www.UnitedNationsForIsrael.org
info@unitednationsforisrael.org

Israel Tours

Travel through Israel on our "Bible Schools on Wheels"
and watch the Hebrew Holy Scriptures come alive.
www.ZionsGospel.com/tours-and-events/

Global Revival MAP (GRM) Israeli Bible Institute

Take the most comprehensive video bible school online that focuses on the restoration of all things.

www.GRMBibleInstitute.com | info@grmbibleinstitute.com

Global Re-Education Initiative (GRI) Against Anti-Semitism

Discover the Jewish Messiah and defeat religious anti-Semitism! Order *The Identity Theft* & GRI Online Course Package

www.Against-Antisemitism.com | info@against-antisemitism.com

From Israel to the Nations TV Programs

Watch Archbishop Dominiquae Bierman's TV programs taped in the land of Israel!

Roku Channel: Israel Revival

YouTube: Dominiquae Bierman TV

www.youtube.com/@DominiquaeBiermanTV

Broadcasting Schedule: www.zionsgospel.com/tv/

MAP Prison Ministry

Through our prison ministry, pioneered by Rabbi Baruch Bierman, GRM Bible School is studied in prisons all over the USA.

More information & to support:

www.zionsgospel.com/map-prison-ministry/

Sign our petition to ban neo-Nazi ideology in America and share it forward!

www.change.org/BanNeoNazism-Evil-Can-Be-Stopped

More Information about the Founder of the Ministries

www.dominiquaebierman.com

B O O K S & M U S I C

For more books by Dr. Dominiquae Bierman,
order online: www.ZionsGospel.com

The Voice of These Ashes
What are the ashes of the exterminated Jewish people crying for?

The Identity Theft
The Return of the 1st century Messiah

Restoring the Glory – Volume I: The Original Way
The Ancient Paths Rediscovered

"Yes!"
The dramatic life story of an Israeli woman who falls
and rises again because of one word: "YES!"

Eradicating the Cancer of Religion
Hint: All people have it!

The Healing Power of the Roots
It's a Matter of Life or Death!

Grafted In
The Return to Greatness

Sheep Nations
It's time to take the nations!

Yeshua is the Name
The Important Restoration of the True Name of the Messiah

The Key of Abraham
The blessing . . . or the curse?

Stormy Weather
Judgment Has Begun and Revival is Knocking at the Doors!

Restoration of Holy Giving
Releasing the True 1,000-Fold Blessing

The MAP Revolution (Free E-Book)
Exposing theologies that obstruct the bride

Vision Negev
The Awesome Restoration of the Sephardic Jews

Defeating Depression
This Book is a Kiss from Heaven

From Sickology to a Healthy Logic
The product of 18 years walking through psychiatric hospitals

ATG: Addicts Turning to God
The Biblical Way to Handle Addicts and Addictions

The Woman Factor
Freedom from Womanophobia
by Rabbi Baruch Bierman with Dominiquae Bierman

The Spider That Survived Hurricane Irma (Free E-Book)
God's call for America to repent

The Revival of the Third Day (Free E-Book)
The Return to Yeshua the Jewish Messiah

Let's Get Healthy, Saints!
The Biblical Guide to Health

Tribute to the Jew in You Music Book
Notes for the Tribute to the Jew in You Music Album

Music Albums
www.ZionsGospel.com

Abba Shebashamayim

Uru

Retorno

The Key of Abraham

Tribute to the Jew in You

Tribute to the Jew in You Instrumental

SUPPORT THE MISSION

Contact Us

www.ZionsGospel.com | shalom@zionsgospel.com

Kad-Esh MAP Ministries

www.Kad-Esh.org | info@kad-esh.org

United Nations for Israel

www.UnitedNationsForIsrael.org
info@unitednationsforisrael.org
52 Tuscan Way, Ste 202-412, St. Augustine,
Florida 32092, USA
+1-972-301-7087

Appendix 4

BIBLIOGRAPHY

Freeman, PhD Joel A, and Griddin, Don B. " Return to Glory",
Destiny Image Publishers, 2003

Koenig, William, "Eye to Eye", About Him Publishing, 2004
Peter, Joel, "Israel And Africa", the British Academic
Press 1992

The Next Frontier Human Development and the Anthropocene
Human Development Report 2020. http://hdr.undp.
org/sites/default/files/hdr2020.pdf

www.ingramcontent.com/pod-product-compliance
Lightning Source LLC
Chambersburg PA
CBHW031222120626
46545CB00003B/953